I'm Finding My Talk

Words by **Rebecca Thomas**

Art by **Pauline Young**

NIMBUS
PUBLISHING
— NIMBUS.CA —

Nimbus Publishing would like to dedicate *I'm Finding My Talk* to the memory of Gregory Younging (1961–2019), Opaskwayak Cree Nation, teacher, editor, and friend, whose work inspired this book. We honour your memory, and your teachings live on.

Nimbus Publishing Limited
3660 Strawberry Hill Street, Halifax, NS, B3K 5A9
(902) 455-4286 nimbus.ca

Printed and bound in Canada
NB1590

Design: Heather Bryan
Editor: Whitney Moran

Library and Archives Canada Cataloguing in Publication

Title: I'm finding my talk / words by Rebecca Thomas ; art by Pauline Young.
Other titles: I am finding my talk
Names: Thomas, Rebecca (Poet), author. | Young, Pauline, 1965- illustrator.
Description: A poem. | Previously published: Halifax, Nova Scotia:
Nimbus Publishing, 2019.
Identifiers: Canadiana 20210128178 | ISBN 9781774710067 (softcover)
Classification: LCC PS8639.H5875 I4 2021 | DDC C811/.6—dc23

Nimbus Publishing acknowledges the financial support for its publishing activities from the Government of Canada, the Canada Council for the Arts, and from the Province of Nova Scotia. We are pleased to work in partnership with the Province of Nova Scotia to develop and promote our creative industries for the benefit of all Nova Scotians.

I want to dedicate this book to my dad, who passed on as much as he could. He taught me what he had left and encouraged me to learn what he couldn't teach. Kesalul.

-RT

This book is dedicated to my father, Phillip Young. May the legacy of his art depiciting Mi'kmaw life live on. I will do my best, Dad.

-PY

I'm finding my talk.
The one I never had.
The one that the schools
Took away from my dad.

Wela'lin

I'm finding my talk
One word at a time.
Kwe
Wela'lin
Nmultes
Sometimes they are very old.
Sometimes they rhyme.

I'm finding my talk
When I'm up on the stage
Telling big stories
Or scribbling words on a page.

I'm finding my talk.

I'm meeting my family.

I'm making new friends,

Who choose to love me.

I'm finding my talk
With clumsy feet
That pat down the grass
With every drumbeat.

I'm finding my talk
With every bead.
My regalia speaks
Through each stitch and seam.

I'm finding my talk.
It's in my smudge bowl,
When the smoke curls around me
And makes me whole.

I'm finding my talk,
How it's written across the land,
Learning to take only what I need.
Netukulimk helps me understand.

I'm finding my talk
Through my community.
From Elders to kids,
This world is still new to me.

I'm finding my talk
By speaking to my father,
By loving him,
By being his daughter.

I'm finding my talk
By speaking with my sister,
Knowing we're different,
And I miss her.

I'm finding my talk
Through my nephews and nieces,
Teaching them they are complete
With all their different pieces.

I'm finding my talk

It's on the inside.

It's how I see the world.

Through not one, but two eyes.

I'm finding my talk
And it may take some time,
But I'm learning to speak
In a language that's mine.

About Rebecca Thomas

REBECCA THOMAS grew up off reserve and outside of her culture. Her father went to residential school and had a hard time teaching Rebecca about her culture because he didn't remember very much about it. He couldn't speak his language anymore and because of that he couldn't teach Rebecca how to speak it either. Rebecca was in her twenties when she read the poem "I Lost My Talk" by Rita Joe and was struck by how much she could relate to it even though she never spoke the language to begin with. Because not only did the Shubenacadie School take away Rita Joe's and Rebecca's father's talk, they took it away from Rebecca, too.

While Rebecca grew up, she had to figure out what it meant to be Mi'kmaq without knowing any of the words for her world. But she started to learn. Rita Joe's work in part inspired Rebecca to use her voice to connect with other Indigenous peoples who are still figuring out who they are and how they fit into a world for which they might not know all the words.

HANNAH JACKSON